Fifty Shades
Of Gravy

The Cookbook

I M Pliant

Published by Sauce Materials

www.saucematerials.com
www.fiftyshadesofgravythecookbook.com

Illustrated by Delme Rosser

ISBN 10: 1480242489
ISBN 13: 978-1480242487

For all lovers of sex and food.

And Mrs Pliant.

Contents

Desserts

Introduction

By the author, I M Pliant

Welcome to Fifty Shades Of Gravy:
The Cookbook.

Oh no, not another cookbook you say.
Or maybe, oh no, not another erotic novel?
Well no, it's neither of those things, except
it's actually both of them. And yet it's so
much more as well. And yet not.

When I was a young man, attempting to
be sexy with some food, I made a terrible
mistake with a banana. I paid for that
mistake dearly, and I wasn't the only one.

Ashamed and frustrated, I was keen to
learn from my experiences. To my surprise
though, there wasn't a single expert, chef
or cookbook out there explaining how to
entertain with, or be entertained by, sexy
food. I was determined to put that right.

But while I was off experimenting, driven by a passion to help people just like me, the world was becoming a more cautious place. We've all been to a dinner party, or at least a Sunday lunch, where things have run their mundane course: the food's boring, the conversation banal, and the Pictionary afterwards an utter anticlimax.

I sincerely hope though, that with the fifty recipes and helpful hints that follow, both "dull dinner" and "sexy food" disasters can become a thing of the past for you, just as they have for me. It's the 21st century after all, so why shouldn't you and your guests be able to enjoy not only some great food, but also some extreme, experimental and passionate lovemaking?

Follow my lead, and people will flock to your gatherings, and the only down side will be the cleaning up afterwards. So, grab a bib, and step inside the delicious world of Fifty Shades Of Gravy.

Let's get messy...

IM Pliant

How To Have A Sexy Dinner Party

Having a successful 'sexy dinner party' is not as simple as inviting round a couple of close friends, ordering a pizza, putting a porno on in the background, and clapping your hands together while saying, "right, who fancies a bunk up?" No, there are do's and don'ts, as with many things in life. And so, as your guide, and based on painful personal experience, here are some basic ground rules to get you started:

Rule No.1
Make sure that your guests know they are attending a sexy dinner party. This is not just so that they know to act 'sexy', it should also inform who you actually invite. For example, don't invite your Nan and Grandad, unless they're into that sort of thing. And in any case, if they are, ewww!

Rule No.2
Select the right kind of mood lighting. If the food is to truly stand a chance of inducing amorous thoughts, neon and spot lighting are not conducive to creating the right atmosphere. Candles, while horribly clichéd, do work. If things are not going well, turn off all the lights and whack on the strobe. A good strobe light can usually create enough confusion and mayhem to lead to all kinds of shenanigans.

Rule No.3

Put on a show. Cutlery and china are important. Paper plates and plastic forks, while easy to dispose of, do evoke a children's party theme and as such, are wholly inappropriate.

Rule No.4

Do it together. Cooking can of course be a solitary pastime - while your guests are laughing and drinking, you are slaving away cutting out glory holes or stewing beef. Nothing is more demoralising than returning with the main course to find you've missed out on all the action. So try and get your guests involved. Perhaps even ask them to help you out, do some chopping, or to put music on. Maybe even to stand in different corners of the room so that temptation doesn't get the better of them. A là Blair Witch.

Rule No.5

Dress right. Ooh what shall I wear? Obviously each dinner will be different, but there are certain rules you might want to follow. For example, never EVER wear rubber while cooking. It's hot and also, in many cases, it's actually some kind of ultra-flammable polyurethane material and goes up like a roman candle if you get hot fat on it.

Rule No.6

Omit fussy eaters. Vegetarians? My advice: keep them away. Experience tells me that only meat eaters have the stamina and disregard for their health to be truly imaginative and fun-filled sexy dinner party guests.

Right, your guests will be here soon, and everyone's really 'hungry'. Let's have a sexy dinner!

Cocktails

A Quick Hand Shandy

A refreshing, earthy, hand-squeezed lemonade and ale shandy

When it comes to speedy refreshment, I would argue furiously that a Quick Hand Shandy beats off all opposition, delivering the unbeatable, instantaneous relief of a cold shower in a glass. What's more, Hand Shandies can be enjoyed anywhere, being just as much fun in the stationery cupboard at work as they are at home when you've gone back to bed to listen to the Today programme after the postman's been.

And whilst a QHS is traditionally taken alone, if a group of strangers I have contacted via the internet want to stand in a circle and watch while I take one in my car, perhaps at a beauty spot just up the road from my house, that's absolutely fine with me.

You will need

1 cup of hot water
½ cup of sugar
1 cup of lemon juice
400ml chilled bitter or ale
A sprig of mint
A twist of fresh ginger

SERVES 1

Let's get messy

To knock off this unusually 'tall' cocktail, heat water in pan • Slowly dissolve sugar and lemon juice to make a cloudy lemon syrup and allow to cool • Pour ale into tankard slowly without tilting, to allow the beer to oxygenate and give you mind-blowing head • Top up with lemon syrup • Add ice and serve with mint and ginger garnish

Fun cocktail tip

As your Hand Shandy is in the making, daydream about jugs – try and serve up a frothy pint's worth in an old man's style dimpled 'jug' glass or 'working man's tankard' (sometimes called a 'Wankard').

Oh, To Cream On A Fuzzy Navel

A Fuzzy Navel ice cream smoothie

I've always thought that sometimes, it's nice to actually see some cream - usually it remains hidden away to minimise mess (and probably to stop us worrying about its ability to 'fatten' us up), but as a result, you do miss out on something which can be creative, highly visual and most enjoyable for those involved.

So, for a rather fantastic, magical way to get your party started, simply pull your secret weapon out of its usual dairy depository (the freezer), smear sweet cream liberally into your guests' fuzzy navels, and watch the expression of joy on their faces.

Cheers!

You will need

1 part peach schnapps
1 part vodka
1 part orange juice
1 part lemonade
1 part vanilla ice cream

SERVES 1

Let's get messy

Blend ingredients and serve in highball glass topped with ice

Fun cocktail tip

If you prefer a more Germanic, 70's style 'Hairy Navel', just add more vodka.

Snowball With The Juice Of A Rum Old Fruit

A twisted Advocaat cocktail with white vintage rum and the juice of a ripe orange

When you take the juice of an old fruit into your mouth, you never know what you're going to get.

But I *guarantee** that your guests will want to swallow this, not run off and spit it out of the window in a gratuitously dramatic fashion, as one of my ex girlfriends did with a cocktail she was not asked to drink in the first place.

(*Not legally binding).

You will need

A handful of ice
2 parts Advocaat
1 part white vintage rum
3 parts ripe orange juice
Chilled lemonade
2 cocktail cherries

SERVES 1

Let's get messy

Put ice into a cocktail shaker and lob in Advocaat, rum and orange juice • Shake well and strain straight into highball or punch-bowl glass • Top up with lemonade, stir, pop your cherries on cocktail sticks, lay across top and serve

Sex And Food Through The Ages: Prehistoric Man

A rudimentary understanding of the history of sexy cooking is a must-have for anyone wishing to cook sexy food or host a dirty dinner party, and that history really all starts with the poor old caveman.

Not renowned for his skills in the kitchen bit of his cave, it was traditionally thought that a diet of fox, dog and snake cooked over an open fire was the height of the caveman's culinary sophistication.

In 1981 however, Professor Pascal Bumtickle (pronounced boom'teck'lay) discovered cave drawings in Nepal that illustrated quite clearly a man proudly holding the penis of a mammoth in one hand and a woman in the other, while standing over what looks like a crude early barbeque.

It's hard to draw definitive conclusions on what this scene depicts, but Bumtickle suggests that this was the first sexy BBQ party, clearly illustrating the man impressing his lady with his ability to barbeque and not burn the penis, but also ensuring her sexual submission to his not inconsiderable manliness.

Canapés

Blue Veiny Cheese Torpedoes

Deep fried Saint Agur potato croquettes

Whenever there's a party, my guests can't wait to get their hands on one of my infamously whiffy blue veined cheese torpedoes. And yes, that's right, you did read that correctly, I don't just give them one: instead, it's bosh, bosh, bosh, and I'm in their face with one torpedo after another after another (three in total).

I like people to leave at the end of the night saying "well that was good Zak / Gladys / Gunther (or whatever), there was certainly more than enough food, nooky etc to go around".

So if you feel the same, my number one tip is to just give freely of your cheese torpedo.

You will need

8 large potatoes peeled and quartered
1 tbsp butter
Seasoning
1 packet Saint Agur cheese
Milk
Flour
1 egg
Breadcrumbs
2 tbsp vegetable oil

SERVES 6-12

Let's get messy

Boil potatoes, mash with butter and season •
Crumble cheese and fold into potato mixture
and whisk over a low heat, adding a little milk
if required • Roll into torpedo shapes and coat
with flour • Beat egg and place in a bowl •
Dip torpedoes into egg, then breadcrumbs,
and fry in pan with hot vegetable oil for 5-7
minutes or until golden

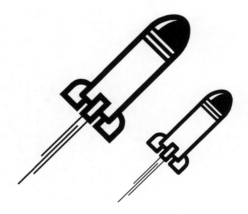

Death By Chocolate Starfish

Star Fruit coated in rich dark Belgian chocolate

The first time your tongue probes the wrinkled centre of a Chocolate Starfish and gives it an almost apologetic lick, you will be amazed.

You might have expected a foul taste, thinking that a Chocolate Starfish plumbs the murkiest depths of the taste ocean, the very bottom.

But it really does work, and that's partly because real, clean, edible starfish are surprisingly hard to get hold of, so what you'll actually be doing is using your imagination, broadening your horizons, and getting to a Chocolate Starfish 'through the back door' via some fruit.

You will need

1-2 star fruit cut into 12 slices
12 cocktail sticks
200g 60% dark chocolate
Greaseproof paper

SERVES 6-12

Let's get messy

Buy ready sliced star fruit or prepare a fresh one •
Break chocolate into small pieces, place in
heatproof bowl set over pan of gently simmering
water and stir until just melted • Line baking tray
with greaseproof paper • Insert cocktail stick in
one end of each star fruit slice and dip one at a
time into chocolate • Place gently on baking sheet
and refrigerate until chocolate is firm • Serve up
your Chocolate Starfish to your astonished guests

Mess-busting food tip

Keep a tissue to hand to wipe off any
excess choccy.

Fun Bags And Sweet Gussets

Decoratively tied paper and poly bags filled with chocs and sweets

It's quite fashionable these days to give your departing dinner party guests the chance to grapple with some fun bags and poly bag gussets filled with sweets.

But why wait until the end of the evening? After all, you want your guests to have a good time, and I think these wonderfully tactile gifts, which can be played with and prodded inexpertly by your guests, are the ultimate 'fun' personal touch.

A lot of people though have contacted me via my website and asked me to explain, in great detail, the difference between fun bags and sweet gussets. Well traditionally, the rule is to offer fun bags when you are not that familiar with your guests, and gussets once you know them better. But I say, life is short; give 'em both, the moment they arrive.

You will need

6 small 'gussets' (poly bags)
6 small squares of coloured tissue paper
Some coloured ribbon cut into ties
Sweets and wrapped chocolates of as many
different varieties as you like

SERVES 6-12

Let's get messy

Divide sweets between poly bags and tissue squares and tie with ribbons • So, not messy at all in fact…

Hot Beef Injections

Moist, plump, pillowy dumplings injected with hot, beefy gravy

If you speak to a professional, they'll dress Hot Beef Injections up as a craft and demand a high price for their services – but the truth is that men and women have been indulging in meat injections for millions of years without fuss or fanfare.

Granted, it can't happen unless you're properly tooled up - your weapon of choice on this occasion being a food syringe, preferably one with a nice thick nozzle – but don't be afraid of the tool, or where it needs sticking.

The absolute worst that can happen is that you end up with a prick on your finger.

You will need

2 rashers smokey back bacon,
chopped up into small pieces
1 onion, chopped
500ml beef stock
Corn flour
250g self-raising flour
125g beef suet, shredded
½ tsp fine sea salt
2 tbsp finely chopped parsley
1 tsp finely chopped rosemary
1 tsp finely chopped thyme
200ml cold water
Food syringe with thick nozzle

SERVES 6-12

Let's get messy

Start by making gravy - fry bacon lardons and onion, then pour in beef stock, and thicken with corn flour as required • Set aside, ready to reheat • Now stick flour in bowl and stir in suet, salt and herbs • Make well in the centre and add enough cold water to mix to soft, spongy dough • Lightly flour your hands and roll the mixture into 12 balls • Boil large pan of water, lower in your balls and cook for 20 minutes • Fill syringe with reheated (caution, warm, not hot) gravy and then inject a tablespoon-full into centre of each still-warm dumpling • If moisture of gravy starts to appear on the surface of dumpling, that's too much • Serve immediately with kitchen towelling to mop up juices

My Incredibly Suckable Nuts

Roasted, toasted nuts with a sugared five spice glaze

I'm told that my sweet but tangy nuts are so tantalisingly suckable that you will want to brush them against your lips, dangle them in your mouth, lick them AND slurp them, all before you finally suck the life out of them until the inside of the nut explodes in your mouth, and you let that juice trickle down your throat, or, if you don't like it, just spit it out into a tissue.

So go on, invite all of your guests to bow down at the altar of (and help themselves to) My Incredibly Suckable Nuts.

You will need

3 cups whole almonds, cashews,
peanuts and pecans
1 cup sugar
4 tsp butter
4 tsp Chinese Five Spice Mix
Sea salt

SERVES 6-12

Let's get messy

Combine ingredients in heavy pan • Cook over medium heat, stirring constantly until sugar is melted and golden in colour, and nuts are toasted (about 7 minutes) • Spread nuts on baking sheet and sprinkle lightly with sea salt

Posh Tarts With Crabs

Crumbly tartlets with fresh crab meat, chives and a mustard lemon mayo

This is a delicate snack you will pay for. Literally.

There are times when we all get a little lonely or down, and over the years, I've discovered that on such occasions there are really only two ways I can cheer myself up.

One is a Hand Shandy, but to be honest I don't always have the 'fodder' at home, and I'm too old to be traipsing down to the corner shop to see what they've got on the shelf.

The other is to pop out for a posh tart, or better still, get one in at home. Be aware though, if you have a partner, they won't thank you for infecting your shared spaces with crabs (EG if they are shellfish intolerant).

You will need

12 small ready made tartlet cases
500g prepared crab meat
175g mayonnaise
½ tbsp French mustard
Juice of ½ lemon
2 tbsp chopped chives
Parmesan
Watercress

SERVES 6-12

Let's get messy

Pre-heat oven to 180c • Mix crab meat, mayo, mustard, lemon and chives together and season with pinch of sea salt and a couple of good twists of black pepper • Fill each tartlet, sprinkle some parmesan on top and pop in oven for five minutes to melt cheese and warm pastry to a fluffy crisp • Serve with watercress garnish

Swollen Purple Bell Ends

Ends of bell peppers with a purple porky bell mushroom stuffing

As a much-loved aunt of mine still says in a gravelly, slightly predatory voice, "it's all about the stuffing".

This particular aunt loves a bell end, and it's the stuffing's wonderfully deep purple hue borne of the combination of deep red beetroots and the blue tinged colouration of good quality organic red cabbage, blended with seasoned pork mince, that really does it for her (longest sentence in book).

NB – if, despite my warnings in my guide on 'How To Have A Sexy Dinner Party', you have agreed to play host to some seasoned non-meat eaters, then do not fret, on this occasion there's no need to stick the pork in.

34

You will need

6 bell peppers
1 tbsp olive oil
1 large onion, finely chopped
2 cloves garlic, finely chopped
200g bell mushrooms, finely chopped
200g pork mince
A handful of breadcrumbs (1-2 slices bread)
2 tbsp chopped flat-leaf parsley
Zest and juice of half a lemon
6 slices of pancetta, halved

SERVES 6-12

Let's get messy

Pre-heat oven to 200c • Heat oil in a large pan and fry onions, garlic and pork mince until softened and gently browned • Add mushrooms and fry until their juices have bubbled away • Stir in breadcrumbs, parsley, lemon zest and juice, season, and remove from heat • Slice lids of bell peppers, lightly oil outsides and then scoop in mix, before placing each bell end back on top and covering with a neatly trimmed pancetta 'lid' to seal the deal • Stick in a baking tray and place in oven for 25-30 minutes or until the peppers look lightly roasted

The Disappointing Chipolata

Runny honey and rustic wholegrain mustard mini-bangers

Who wants a chipolata when a jumbo, king-size sausage is available?
Well, actually, the answer is that plenty of people do, alright? So the name is ironic.

Whilst there's no doubt a big sausage has some sort of lowest common denominator 'battering ram' appeal, the true sausage fiend knows that a little one works harder for your love, and in the hands of a master, can be a wizard's wand.

My recommendation for a party is to dip your chipolatas in honey and (go with me on this) mustard, before you offer them to guests – that way, whilst they may titter at your teensy offering, once they've had a nibble they will take you very seriously indeed.

You will need

24 chipolatas
2 tbsp clear honey
2 tbsp wholegrain mustard
250ml sour cream
½ tsp paprika
A sprig of mint

SERVES 6-12

Let's get messy

Pre-heat oven to 200c • Mix honey and mustard and smear on tiny sausages • Cook for 25 mins or until cooked through and crisp on outside • Mix together the sour cream, paprika and mint and place in a dipping bowl, and serve alongside your mini porkers

Sex And Food Through The Ages: The Romans

It's widely known that the Romans enjoyed orgies, but did you know the first orgy started in a kitchen? They were of course far less sophisticated than we are today but according to ancient tablets documenting the times, written by Roman senator Grabbus Maximus, the fashion for rude food started back in the days of togas, laurel wreathes and all that shit.

Grabbus said in 37BC: "The kitchen fire started in the pantry where the cook, Gluttonous Fatuous kept the cheese. He struck upon the idea of melting cheese into crude shapes for the guests of my friend Dirtius Helmetus. After rubbing ourselves with oil, we started on appetisers of baked dormice testes followed by donkey nostrils covered in clam juice. However, once the wine arrived, men and women feasted on giraffe penises and lamb vaginas with a side salad and then it got all sexy and it was an orgy. It was brilliant".

Light Bites

Big, Hard, Well Hung Sausage With Baby Batter

Kingsize 28 day beef sausage fried with an irresistible Babycham batter

A bloated, well hung piece of beef, left to its own devices for a month – now that is going to explode in your mouth, and with the unique taste of my baby batter following it down your gullet, this is quite the beef treat for lovers of a big greasy sausage.

Note well though: you must avoid battering Mr Sausage too assertively to be rewarded with something that is crispy to the touch, and greasy enough to taste lovely and go down easy, but not so greasy as to leave a stain if pressed against kitchen towelling.

You will need

6 28-day beef sausages
(size does matter)
Long skewers
375ml Babycham
100g corn flour
100g plain flour
1 pinch salt
1 tsp grated lemon zest
Vegetable oil
A bowl of plain flour
Ketchup or aioli

SERVES 6

Let's get messy

Fry (or do as the BBQ-ing Aussies would and boil) sausages until cooked through • Pierce with skewers for remainder of the preparation • Combine flour, salt, lemon zest and Babycham and whisk to a batter • Heat 5cm of vegetable oil to 180c in a high-sided pan. Check temperature by dropping a small cube of bread into it: it should become golden and crispy in 1 minute • Dust sausages in plain flour, dip into batter and then deep fry for 3-5 minutes • Wipe excess grease off your sausage and serve with ketchup or aioli

Hot Cock On Baps

A spicy spatchcock chicken served with soft, crusty, oven-fresh baps

This is a simple yet undeniably perfect end to a romantic, rainy Sunday at home. It's succulent, and it's smoochy. Ergo, it's also ideal for a sexy dinner party.

Simply get a cock really hot and then smear its juices all over a nice petite pair of baps or even some large, squidgy buns: yep, those baps will be soggy, but what better way is there to mop up the tangy taste of all that succulent, delicious cock fat?

One word of warning though: when it comes to baps and buns, DO take precautions and do NOT make the mistake of letting things get too heated.

It is easy to get distracted when someone is waving hot cock in your face, but there is a huge risk you will be left with a bun in the oven.

You will need

1 spatchcock (1.5kg)
1 tsp ground cinnamon
1 tsp smoked paprika
1 tsp ground cumin
1 tsp ground coriander
1 clove garlic, crushed
1 pinch chilli flakes
1-2 tbsp olive oil

SERVES 6

Let's get messy

Prepare chicken and slash thick parts of legs and thighs with sharp knife • Mix marinade and rub all over your bird, working into each gash • Place in large sealable bag or plastic container and leave to marinate for at least 3 hours, preferably overnight • Needlessly repeat the word 'gash' • Pre-heat oven to 180c • Heat griddle pan until very hot and sear chicken on each side until it has nice charred lines, then place in oven for 45 minutes, or until crispy brown and cooked through

Necrophiladelphia Cheese Sandwiches

Dead sexy Stilton and cream cheese sandwiches with walnut and pear

These delicious double-dosed cheese sandwiches use rotting blue cheese - which I always like to think carries the unmistakable stench of death and decay - to complement the 'safe' velvet smoothness of branded cream cheese.

To cheer up what can be a rather sombre sarnie, finish them off according to taste with some brown crinkly walnuts, a nice juicy pear, or both, making them ideal for wakes and swingers' parties alike.

You will need

½ cup toasted walnuts
100g Stilton
1tsp tarragon
1 small shallot, chopped
1 pear
One sourdough loaf
200g cream cheese, go for a reputable brand

SERVES 6

Let's get messy

Crumble your nuts in a bowl with Stilton, tarragon and shallot • Peel, core and slice pear thinly • Slice sourdough, spread cream cheese on bread and then place Stilton mix and pear slices in between layers • Cut into small, dainty triangles and serve with a creepy leer

The Soft, Warm English Muffin

The traditional yeasty delight of warm and yielding sweet English bun

There'll always be an England. Renowned for our inhibited sexual behaviour, when we do get going, decades of repression spew out like Niagara Falls.

The Soft Warm English Muffin is an evocative, old fashioned, almost mythical indulgence – there's even a whiff of Dickens about it. I can just imagine a warm English Muffin being sold on the streets of London in the 1880s like a common whore – a useful and evocative image to share whilst dishing them up at a luncheon.

Your muffin will have to be kneaded to make it sufficiently pliable, and then simply split it with butter while it's still hot for a wonderfully simple, hugely under-rated treat.

You will need

Small packet of dried yeast
250ml water
225g natural yoghurt
250ml of milk
750g plain flour
2 tbsp of caster sugar
A pinch of salt
Semolina
50g butter
Oil, for greasing

SERVES 4-6

Let's get messy

Mix half the water and the yeast until they have become one • Add rest of the water to creamy yoghurt • Add yeasty liquid to sieved flour and add salt • Knead it. Go on. That's it. It loves it. Look how it yields to your touch • Put it in a bowl and cover it in Clingfilm or a wipe clean sheet • Leave to stand and admire your work for 30 minutes • Take it out. Knead it again. Roll it in your hands so that it's about 2cm thick • Cut the now fully submissive dough into round shapes. Don't worry, it likes it • Place it on a baking tray dusted with flour and bake for 40 minutes • Watch them rise again • Cook half the muffins in frying pan, but be careful not to overdo it • Remove snooker ball gag from your mouth • Cook the other muffins in frying pan • Serve hot to your guests with lots of butter and a weird smile.

Fun food suggestion

Give the whole thing a Victorian feel by eating by gaslight and standing in the corner of the room in a tall top hat and large moustache, judging your diners.

Two Birds, One Cup

A duck and chicken roasted delight in a thick gravy

The internet is an invention that has truly changed the way the world works. So much knowledge means that the world has become a smaller place, a place where information is readily available on government conspiracies and the latest news from around the world, and voices are heard that previously would have been silent, plus loads of shockingly disgusting porn is now easily accessible.

So in tribute to that latter phenomenon, I present to you, Two Birds, One Cup, and ask you to try and put out of your mind the real thing if you have seen it. This is really quite simple: find two contrasting game birds, get a cup of gravy, and pour it over them. Dirty birds.

You will need

A whole chicken
A whole duck
Salt and pepper
Oil
2 onions
2 sprigs of thyme
1 cup of gravy
Greens
A knob of butter

SERVES 4-6

Let's get messy

Pre-heat oven to 200c • Season your birds with salt and pepper • Oil them up • Slam them into an oven dish with the onion and thyme • Bake them for 70-90 minutes or until roasted and cooked through • Remove and cover with your cup of hot gravy • Serve with buttered greens

Important food tip

Do NOT search for this on the internet, unless you have a strong stomach. Or ate a good while ago. Or are using someone else's computer.

Sexy Food:
The Blacklist

Whilst it's great, just great, to let your imagination run wild when 'sexy cooking', some foods should be studiously avoided.

Here's a list of items you should never in any circumstances use in sex on account of them not being sexy:

Sandwiches
Scotch eggs
Bovril
Corn flakes
Chewing gum
Marrows
Corned beef
Biltong
Pilchards or mackerel
Cornish pasties
Baked beans
Curry
Raw liver
Raw onions
Camembert
Pickled onions
Crisps (especially Wotsits and Monster Munch)
Anything boil in the bag
Bombay mix
Lemon juice

Big Dinners

Anything With A Pulse

A warming, aromatic winter pulse stew with Indian spices

Chicks, broads, even mungs - I'll nosh anything with a pulse. If it's hot, all the better, but I ain't bothered.

If you fancy a root (EG carrot or parsnip) or some meat (EG lamb), be my guest and squeeze it in. But this dish was designed as a challenge to a good friend of mine, Negative Pauline, to prove a point: that you and your guests should be able to dine out on Anything With A Pulse, and walk away sated.

You will need

1 tbsp vegetable, groundnut or coconut oil
1 large onion, chopped
1 chilli, chopped
1 lump fresh ginger, grated
2 cloves garlic, chopped
2 tsp garam masala
1 can chickpeas drained and rinsed
½ cup dried red lentils
½ cub black eyed beans
½ cup canned kidney beans
1 tin of chopped tomatoes
500ml vegetable stock
100ml plain yoghurt
Coriander as garnish

SERVES 6

Let's get messy

Pre-heat oven to 130c • Heat oil in a heavy-bottomed oven-proof pan and sauté onions • Add chilli, ginger, garlic and garam masala and lightly fry until onions soften • Add pulses, tinned tomatoes and vegetable stock and cook for 6 hours, adding more stock if needed • Gently fold in yoghurt 5 minutes before you finish cooking, garnish with fresh coriander, and serve with wild rice or Bombay potatoes

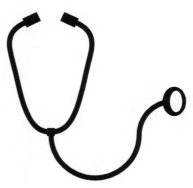

Auntie Sue's Bearded Clam Chowder

(aka Hairy Pie)

A fragrant and creamy family favourite - fish stew with angel hair pasta

I have a wonderful photo of my uncle Toby, a slathering great big slob, wearing long safari shorts, a pith helmet and a large bib, chowing down on my Auntie Sue's famous Bearded Clam.

Great times - and I wish you great times as well with this intercontinental fusion of Clam Chowder and Spaghetti Ai Frutti Di Mare – a New England chowder with extra oomph thanks to the addition of angel hair pasta.

58

You will need

30 clams
100g butter
2 onions, finely sliced
2 rashers of bacon
1 stick celery, sliced
1 carrot, diced
A splash of white wine
100g angel hair pasta
1 large potato, cubed
300ml milk
300ml cream
Bay leaf
Salt
Parsley

SERVES 6

Let's get messy

Wash clams and place in a large pan with a couple of cm of water • Cover and cook on hob until they're open, then remove from heat and drain the liquid/clam juice into a cup or bowl • Wait for clams to cool then remove from shells and cut meat into smaller pieces • Heat butter in a large frying pan, add onions, bacon, celery and carrot, and sweat until lightly browned • Add wine and cook this off • At same time, plunge pasta into boiling salty water and cook until barely al dente; remove and drain • Put potatoes, milk, cream and bay leaf in large pan and bring to the boil, then simmer until just cooked • Shout 'clam juice' nine or ten times, starting at a whisper, ending at a scream; add rest of the ingredients, warm through and season as required • Serve garnished with chopped parsley

Fun food fact

You don't have to use actual bearded clams (clams without the beard removed), but clams (bearded or otherwise) can also be served with 'Puttanesca' sauce, which translates as 'whore's pasta'. What fun!

Boned Bird, Tied Up And Stuffed With Sausage

A whole plump, roast duck cooked with onions, and stuffed with sausage meat

Some birds don't have a lot of meat on the bone, yet many people these days are admitting that they like a bit more of a handful. One way to get the plumpness you desire is to stuff your bird, in this case duck, with sausage meat.

Get your butcher to bone your bird, if you like that sort of thing - it's quite good fun to watch a hefty tattooed man go to town on your bird.

After that, it's yours. Do what you want with it. Punish it. Admonish it. Perhaps you'll just sit at the kitchen table staring at it. Shaking your head and telling it you "didn't think it was capable of such things"

Alternatively, stuff it…

You will need

1 whole boned duck
4 sausages, use flavoured ones
to make things more interesting
1 onion
1 cooking apple
1 cup of nuts
(walnuts are traditional)
Parsley, chopped

SERVES 6

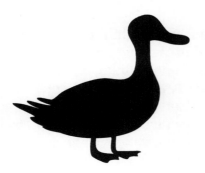

Let's get messy

Wipe the duck down. It's been bad, it needs to be cleaned. Then slam it skin down onto a board and season it with salt and pepper • Pre-heat oven to 200c • Squeeze the meat from the sausages. This is about the most fun you can have in the kitchen with your clothes on, and besides, who said you need to be clothed? • Mix the sausage meat with the onion and apple (which you should have chopped) and walnuts too • Then form the whole thing into a gigantic sausage shape • Insert your giant spicy sausage into your bird (in some cases, your bird may need to be wrapped round the sausage) • Tie your bird up with string where you inserted the sausage • Roast the bird for about an hour and a half • Lay the bird on the table

Complimentary food tip

Stuffing a bird moistens it to make service much easier, so don't forget to invite some guests. It's often good to serve the bird with buttered greens, roast potatoes and some fruity sauce.

Feeding The Ducks With A Five Knuckle Shuffle

A knuckle of beef sliced into five, filled with foie gras, tied up and roasted

I perfected this when I was single, developing ever more elaborate ways of pulling it off – in the end I could do it standing on my head.

So when a weekend fishing trip companion called Alan suggested I not contact him for a while and perhaps think about reviving this in private, I needed no encouragement to get further practice in and check out new ways of doing it on the internet.

Fortuitously, my wife was giving me the cold shoulder at the time (not a cold shoulder of beef unfortunately!!!!!!), so I was able to thrash away at some good hard uninterrupted research whilst Jeremy Kyle was on, my favourite time of the day for preparing something 'off the cuff'.

You will need

6 thick beef knuckle steaks
2 jars of foie gras pate or parfait
Kitchen twine
Paprika
Seasoning
Olive oil

SERVES 6

Let's get messy

Pre-heat oven to 220c • Lay knuckles flat and season • Spread foie gras thickly on each side of the steaks, except the two 'outer' surfaces • Rack your steaks together and tie up with kitchen twine • Season again, and sprinkle with paprika • Briefly sear on all sides in an oiled griddle pan and then place into oven and cook for 25 minutes or until beef is cooked to your preference

Force Meat In The Hole

A Toad in the Hole, using best 'forcemeat' instead of sausage

If I do say so myself, and I do say so (myself), this is a great idea: for those not keen on having their hole filled with toad, force meat in there instead.

It revolutionises this dish and will revolutionise your life, with its smooth pleasures of high quality meat slipped into your light, fluffy batter, all moistened with a jus or gravy.

Yummy.

You will need

3 tbsp parsley, chopped
1 tbsp rosemary, chopped
250g onions, chopped
350g sausage meat
1 goose liver, chopped
Seasoning
3 free-range eggs
185g plain flour
125ml milk mixed with 150ml cold water
1½ tbsp grain mustard
4 tbsp lard

SERVES 6

Let's get messy

Pre-heat oven to 220c • Combine parsley, rosemary, onions, sausage meat, goose liver and seasoning and blend briefly to a thick paste in a food mixer, before molding into large sausagey dong shapes • Sprinkle your 'sausages' with flour and then give them a quick sizzle in a frying pan to cement their aforementioned dong shapes • Whisk together eggs, flour, milk, mustard and more seasoning to the consistency of double cream • Rest for 15 minutes – the mixture, not you • Put lard in a roasting tin and pop it in oven until smoking – the lard, not you • Pour in batter - it will sizzle softly in the hot fat - then arrange sausages in batter • Transfer tin back into the oven and bake for 25 minutes until puffed and golden • Serve with gravy

Fun Food Presentation Idea #1 Bukkake Moussaka

You can make quite an impression when hosting a sexy dinner gathering if you employ some creative presentation ideas – and here's a great one.

Bukkake is that ancient Japanese tradition of admonishing a wife's suspected adultery by inviting a bunch of friends over to…well. There's no need for me to expand on this, but suffice to say, everyone, especially the wife, needs a long shower afterwards.

Moussaka is an ancient Greek / Turkish / Balkan casserole that combines aubergines vegetables and lamb mince. It's tasty and only one thing could make it better: needlessly combining it with a Japanese fetish activity where a woman is the centre of attention. And not in a good way.

In this particular recipe, Bukkake is in fact a whole can of fun for all your guests to enjoy.

You will need

A pinch or two of cinnamon
1 clove of garlic
750g lamb mince
1 large tin of chopped tomatoes
1 onion
1 bay leaf
2 aubergines
Salt and pepper
4 medium sized potatoes,
peeled and cooked
1 tsp chopped oregano
75g butter, 2 eggs, flour and
Gruyere cheese for topping
Four cans of squirty cream

Let's get messy

Brown mince, and cook onion till translucent •
Slice and brown aubergines and combine with
mince and onions • Add garlic, tomatoes, bay leaf,
oregano • Season with salt and pepper • Make
sauce by heating butter, whisking eggs and adding
flour and cheese • Add mince etc to an ovenproof
dish, top with potatoes, and top that with the sauce
• Cook it for half an hour or until brown on top

Now, bukkake that moussaka!

Give each of the guests a can of squirty cream •
Each must stand at the same distance from the
moussaka • All of you shake the cans at waist
height (this is an important visual effect) •
Squirt the cream onto the top of the moussaka

Tip

Do make sure you have enough cans to hand
around to each guest. There's nothing quite so
pathetic as one of your guests stood slightly
outside your ring of cream, looking on forlornly
as the rest of you squirt your loads onto the dish.

Game
For
Anything
Pie

A surprising and tasty pie combining a variety of game birds with tasty vegetables

You know that feeling? That feeling when, maybe you've had a couple of glasses of wine and you feel a little carefree? Perhaps you just feel that things have been a bit boring of late. That they need "livening up". Well this could be the pie for you. It's a pie that looks at you excitedly and says, "Yeah, go on, I'll give it a go. Why the hell not?!"

Pies don't need to be predictable, they can spring a surprise or two, and with this particular concoction, there's a delightful bombshell in every mouthful. A delicious dish for the more daring dinner party (ie one where you expect to do a lot of shagging).

You will need

1.25kg various bits of game e.g.
grouse, pheasant, pigeon, quail,
venison, duck, partridge, chopped
50g plain flour
2 large red onions, chopped
1 clove garlic, crushed
200g mushrooms, chopped
2 tbsp cranberries, crushed
1 glass of port or hefty red wine
250ml chicken stock
300g puff pastry
1 egg, beaten
Salt and pepper

SERVES 4-6

Let's get messy

Get a pie dish. It's important you have one of these
• Oil the pie dish • Coat meat in flour and oil •
Season with salt and pepper • Brown meat in
casserole dish • Add onions and mushrooms and
soften • Keep stirring with your big spoon •
Add stock, but keep a little back to serve it with •
Cover and cook in an oven for about for 90 mins •
Make the pastry into a pie • Spoon in the meat
filling • Put the pie lid on top • Bake it for about
half an hour • Serve

Helpful food tip

As the name suggests, this is a dish that should
be served to adventurous and open-minded
guests. And naive ones too of course.

Gently Jerked Pork

Best pork chops with a subtle jerk seasoning, served with rice and peas

Jerked pork exploded onto the food scene in this country about ten years ago, but in truth, much of what you got could only be described as a load of rank old bone, jerked to kingdom come.

Fans of cock will know that it's nigh on impossible to choke chicken with jerk - it can take this kind of flavour-assault without being overwhelmed.

The trick with a tender, flaccid piece of pork though, is to not jerk it too ferociously, as this can result in both bruising and so called 'premature ejerkulation', where you overload your meat with flavours too early on in the process, making it far less satisfying.

You will need

6 pork chops
225g onions, quartered
1-1½ scotch bonnets halved and seeded
50g root ginger, peeled and chopped
½ tsp ground allspice
Handful fresh thyme leaves
1 tsp black pepper
120ml white wine vinegar
120ml dark soy sauce

SERVES 6

Let's get messy

Blend marinade ingredients and place in sealable food bags with the chops, and leave overnight •
Roast in a 200c oven for 25 minutes or until the pork is cooked through and crisping nicely •
Serve with salad, rice and peas

Hide
The
Sausage

A huge party size 'bucket' of cheesy, herb mash, with one 'secret sausage' hidden somewhere inside…

Men and women having been hiding the sausage since dinosaur days (ish) and from your first time as a nervous teenager, to when as Grandma and Grandad you roll back the years in your 90s, it never fails to delight.

That said, the simplest things are sometimes the easiest to get wrong, so TAKE YOUR TIME. We have all experienced a rushed Hide The Sausage, and women in particular have frequently told me what a frustrating disappointment I am, sorry it is, to them.

Get it right though, and it is, quite simply, a fun dish with a sausage.

You will need

One large beef or pork sausage
12 large potatoes
1 tbsp butter
3 tbsp single cream
Seasoning
100g freshly grated cheddar
100g freshly grated parmesan
1 handful of chives, finely chopped
1 cup of full cream milk

SERVES 6

Let's get messy

Fry your sausage until it is cooked through and crisping on the outside • Keep warm in a low oven • Peel, boil and drain your spuds • Replace back into pan, mix in butter, cream and seasoning, place on low heat • Stirring rapidly, blend in cheese and chives, and mix in as much of the milk as you require to get the ideal 'mash' consistency

Sausage tip

Serve as a meal and a dinner party game in one - whoever finds the sausage, faces a fun food forfeit (to be discussed and agreed in advance complete with 'safe words').

Hot Fish Sausage, Doggy Style

A spicy seafood sausage made with dogfish (shark)

Some people will find this demeaning, and I admit, there's not much in it for the dogfish. But if you write this off as caveman territory, I think you are missing a trick.

I actually think dogfish (which is basically shark), or even rock salmon, which is an excellent alternative for this recipe, like getting rigorously sausaged once in a while. I have absolutely no evidence for this – it's pure speculation.

You will need

400g dog fish or rock salmon fillets
200g coley
75g breadcrumbs
1 egg white
1 shallot, grated
1 tbsp fresh fennel, chopped
1 tsp chilli powder
Seasoning
Butter
Sourdough bread
Rocket
Mayonnaise

SERVES 6

Let's get messy

Combine the fish, breadcrumbs, egg white, shallot, fennel and chilli; season and then blend in a food mixer until consistent but still rough • Shape into 8 humorous sausage shapes, wrap each in cling-film and foil and then store in the fridge for 45 minutes to help maintain their shape • Poach sausages in simmering water (still in Clingfilm and foil) for 15-20 minutes • Lightly brown in a buttered pan then serve with bread, rocket and mayonnaise

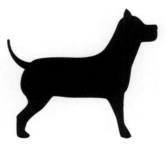

I Feel Like Chicken Breasts Covered In Cum Juice Tonight

Chicken breasts with a cumquat and herb stuffing basted with delicious cumquat juice

Uh, uh, uh...aaaaaaahhhh! I have to admit that I am really not that experienced in such matters, but I have always imagined that this would be the sound made by someone who has just got cum juice all over some breasts, possibly their own.

Whatever though, this really is a delicious combination which is an absolute delight to prepare, as you knead the sweet, sticky, seedy cum juices into the chicken fillets or breasts. Maybe invite your guests to watch.

You will need

6 free range chicken breasts
300g cumquats, chopped
40cl sugar syrup
185g unsalted butter, softened
½ cup fresh parsley, roughly chopped
6 sprigs lemon thyme,
stripped and chopped
Seasoning

SERVES 6

Let's get messy

Pre-heat oven to 200c • Make an incision in chicken breasts for stuffing and set aside • Place chopped cumquats and sugar syrup into a small saucepan, place over medium heat and boil for 5 minutes • Remove cumquats into a mixing bowl, but leave juice in pan • Add syrup, butter, parsley, thyme, and seasoning to cumquats, mix, and stuff each breast • Roast for approximately 20 minutes or until chicken is cooked through • Remove from oven and serve with some of the warmed pan juices, alongside buttered spuds and purple sprouting broccoli. Voilà – you've got cum juice all over your breasts

Lick My Spuds, Butter My Carrot, Shank Me Off

Tender lamb shank roast cooked with gravy, buttered veg and crispy roast potatoes

There's no meat tastier or more tender than a lamb shank. It slides off the bone so easily, and what better way to accompany it than with some lightly buttered carrots and potatoes with just a lick of semolina to make them crispy.

This dish is like a personalised roast where you get the meat all to yourself.
You lucky dog. A particularly simple and straightforward dish. No messing about, just a good old fashioned shank, with the inevitable lashings of gravy.

You will need

2 lamb shanks
2 onions, chopped
4 potatoes
Semolina
Season
200g carrots
½ white cabbage
50g butter
250ml lamb / onion gravy

SERVES 2

Let's get messy

Pre-heat oven to 200c • Take your two lamb shanks and place them in oiled up baking tin • Pour half gravy over them • Cover in chopped onions • Cook in oven for 30 minutes • Meanwhile, peel your potatoes and parboil • Drain water and bash your spuds in pan to make them fluffy spuds • Sprinkle semolina liberally over potatoes • Season with salt and pepper • Put into tin with the lamb shanks and cook for 45 minutes • Put the carrots in about halfway through • Steam the cabbage • Serve with the rest of the gravy

Really great food tip

The best place to get a quality shank is at your butcher's. Simply walk in and declare that you need a shank. Probably two in fact. Ask him if you should come out the back to get them. Perhaps offer a friendly wink as you do.

Ten Sexy Snacks For The Lonely Man

Melon with a hole cut into it

Any sponge pudding except spotted dick

Two slices of ham

Bowl of jelly with a cherry on top

Vertically served pitta bread with lettuce filling and a single olive at the top

Tub of cottage cheese

Jar of jam (apricot is nicest)

Kebab

Sashimi (avoid that hot, green stuff)

A plate of mashed potato

Milked Sausage And Balls

Boudin Blanc sausage and German milky meatballs

Boudin Blanc is a delicious French blood milk sausage. Sure, that sounds delicious, but clearly it's also a recipe that requires you to grind your own meat. "Oh no, that sounds like a nightmare" I hear the faint-hearted cry!

But please, don't worry. If you want someone else to milk your sausage, Boudin Blanc are available at exceptionally good deli's (if you live in Stoke or something, that's not my problem) - or you can simply buy chipolatas and they'll become 'milky by osmosis' (which is a great name for a band) when cooked in close proximity to the milky German balls.

You will need

500g ground beef
Seasoning
1 tsp dill (dried)
200g dry breadcrumbs
250ml milk
1 tbsp chopped parsley
1 egg (slightly beaten)
250ml thick beef stock
100g sliced mushrooms, drained
1 onion, chopped
4 Bouidin Blanc or 8 chipolatas
250ml sour cream
250ml single cream
1 tbsp flour

SERVES 6

Let's get messy

Mix together ground beef, salt and pepper, dill, breadcrumbs, milk, parsley and egg • Shape into 24 meatballs • Brown slowly in a large, lightly oiled pan • Add beef stock, mushrooms and onions • Cover, and simmer for 30 minutes • Take out meatballs • Blend together creams and flour, and stir into broth • Add meatballs and sausages, stir, bring to the boil and simmer for 5 minutes • Serve over German dumplings, noodles or mashed potatoes

Fun food fact

The German for meatballs is Kummel Klops. Klops sounds a bit like plop, so it's a bit like 'Cum Plops' really.

Overdoing
The Rabbit

Slow cooked rabbit stew

I love a dish with a story behind it, and this one simply buzzes with social history. In leaner times where meat, even cheap and ordinarily readily available sausage, was hard to come by, the women and wives of Great Britain traditionally turned to the rabbit.

It has always been possible to overdo the rabbit though, spending hours beavering away so that what you ultimately end up with is a bruised and dried up husk. But as we've grown more sophisticated, what we've come to understand is that by turning down the dial a bit, you can stick the rabbit in for several hours, and end up with the most satisfying, orgasmic end result.

You will need

40ml brandy
50g soft brown sugar
50g pitted prunes
2 rabbits, jointed
2 tbsp plain flour
1 tbsp olive oil
3 rashers streaky bacon, chopped
2 carrots, chopped
1 celery stick, chopped
1 onion, chopped
1 garlic clove, crushed
2 thyme sprigs
1 bay leaf
150ml red wine
250ml chicken stock
A small handful of parsley

SERVES 6

Let's get messy

Pre-heat oven to 140c • Combine brandy, brown sugar and prunes then set aside to soak • Dust rabbit in flour and then brown in a casserole dish • Set rabbit aside • Add bacon, vegetables, garlic and herbs to the casserole and fry gently for 5 mins • Add the wine, chicken stock, rabbit and prune mix then cover and cook for 4 hours, stirring occasionally, until the rabbit is totally tender • Garnish with parsley and serve with mashed potatoes on the side

Shepherd's Bi-Curious Cottaging Pie

A beef and lamb pie - familiar yet strange, and utterly delicious

Am I a Shepherd's Pie? Am I a Cottage Pie? Why can't I be both? That's the question answered with this dish as the shepherd goes cottaging in this pie-brid.

It's a lonely life herding any animal, and so a nice warm pie would be one way of keeping a shepherd occupied. Much to the delight of the sheep. With the Shepherd's Bi-Curious Cottaging Pie you get two dishes for the price of one. It is a pie, but it's also a pies.

You will need

250g minced lamb
250g minced beef
Seasoning
100g carrots, diced
1 onion
2 tsp of tomato puree
1 tsp nutmeg
1 tbsp Worcestershire sauce
500g potatoes, chopped
Salt and pepper
70g butter
250ml milk

SERVES 4

Let's get messy

Pre-heat oven to 200c • Brown both seasoned minces and add onions and carrots and soften • Add puree, nutmeg and Worcestershire sauce and remove into an ovenproof dish • Boil your spuds • Mash them, adding butter and milk as you do • Top mince with the mash, fluffing as you go • Bake for 25 mins

Storage warning

This dish can be frozen for up to a month before cooking in the oven. But that's not very sexy. Freezers aren't sexy.

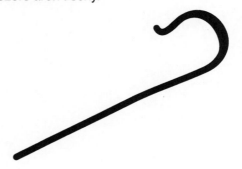

Up To The Nuts In Guts

A delicious offal pie with a topping of sweet sprinkled nuts

How deep? Nut deep! Guts, or offal, have made a haute cuisine comeback as the middle class "go authentic" and start eating war food again. Spam fritters anyone?

Offal does get a bad press. It's a bit like your first time doing sex. The thought or sight of things can actually be disgusting, and if you delve too deep into the detail of it, it's quite off putting really. But come on, man/woman up about this. You like meat? So what's wrong with guts?

Offal's just a blanket term for anything that the butcher wouldn't usually give to his dog. It comes from a word meaning meat that the poor could afford. However, some cuts can be very healthy, so next time someone tells you that "being up to the nuts in guts all the time isn't healthy", you can employ a wry smile.

You will need

1kg offal cuts; kidney, liver, heart,
or simply ask the butcher for some tripe
Seasoning
Oil
3 onions
300ml thick beef stock
A packet of puff pastry
100g mixed nuts
100g garden peas
250ml beef stock
Salt and pepper

SERVES 4

Let's get messy

Pre-heat oven to 200c • Brown your seasoned meat in a pan with oil • Add the onions until lightly cooked • Top up with the stock, bring to the boil then place in an ovenproof dish and cook for 25 minutes • Make the pie base from the pastry, fill with the meat and onion • Sprinkle your nuts over the top of the pie and cook in the oven for another 25 minutes • Serve with peas

Fun food suggestion

Why not try 'Up To The Nuts In Guts In An Old Boiler'? As above but cooked in an old 'boiler' cooker for that retro feel.

Fun Food Presentation Idea #2 Roasted Bone Marrow, Doggy Style

Are you a captain of industry? Do you manage lots of people and say things like "it's my way or the highway" or "come on people, let's work 10% harder yeah"?

If you are, then after a hard day's work lording it over your minions, you probably like nothing more than to be degraded and treated like the soulless dog you are.

You've worked hard all your life and you've commanded respect in your professional life, you deserve the abuse which you so dearly crave. Are you sick? Not sick as such, more a hopelessly predictable wretch.

So that's it, eat up your dinner Fido, get on all fours and eat it out of the bowl.

You bad dog!

You will need

1 dog bowl
Beef bone marrow, cut into pieces
1 garlic clove (crushed)
2 onions (sliced)
1 parsley sprig
4 slices of French bread
Salt and pepper

Down boy

Roast the marrow bones for about 20 minutes •
Add the onions and garlic and season with salt and
pepper • Scoop out the bone marrow and spread it
on some lovely French bread, add a sprig of
parsley for presentation and then dump it in the
dog bowl

Doggy tip

Sure, you're on all fours, and sure, you should be
wearing a lead (that's right Americans, not a
leash). But how about a nice drink to go with that
yeah? Put a metal bowl next to your dinner and fill
it with water. Lap it up, you silly dog.

Desserts

A Lovely Juicy Pair Of Melons, A Couple Of Creamy Jugs And Two Great Big Wobblers

(also known as a Sixtit)

Cantaloupe melons served with twin jugs of fresh cream and two jellies

Aaah – who doesn't love melons?
OK, so some prefer a banana, and who can blame them, but I've got a recipe that will win over even the most hardened nana-phile. Grab your melons, and simply whop them out. And that's pretty much it! Served this way, au naturel, they are impossible to resist.

Some people - idiots I call them - claim melons are incomplete without a bit of undercooked Italian meat thrust between them, but I simply do not subscribe to that school of pork thought. Instead, relish in the simplicity and symmetry by completing your dinner display with two great big jugs of cream and a couple of wobblers, or 'jellies'.

You will need

2 cantaloupe melons
300ml single cream
300ml whipping cream
2 packets of jelly
4 maraschino cherries

SERVES 4-6

Let's get messy

Set the jellies in separate bowls – when ready, remove onto a serving dish and place a halved cheery atop each half, like a funny nipple • Halve the melons – remove seeds. Turn skin-side up and place a halved cheery atop each half, also like a funny nipple • Whip cream and place in one jug, and pour single cream into other jug

Top sixtit tip

Give each guest a bowl, a spoon and an invitation to wobble their face in the Sixtit before they tuck in – there's plenty to go around

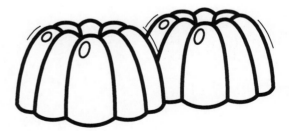

Banana Turnover Surprise

(With Chocolate Banana)

A pastry turnover filled with sticky, chocolate banana

When I first served this up to my wife –
well, boy did she ever turn round and give
me a puzzled look over her shoulder.

That is the beauty of being on the end of
the Turnover Surprise – that unexpected
little jolt of surprise that gets you every time.

And the giver/caterer too for that matter:
you agree to serve up a turnover, you
realise you are failing to locate the fruit you
had in mind (EG peach), and before you
know it, you are dipping a banana in
chocolate. Surprising.

You will need

1 frozen puff pastry sheet, thawed
Butter
Milk
1 egg, beaten
3-4 bananas
Branded chocolate hazelnut spread

SERVES 6

Let's get messy

Pre-heat oven to 200c • Unfold thawed pastry sheet on a lightly floured surface and cut into six 10x10 cm squares • Spread one surface of each square thickly with the branded hazelnut spread • Slice your banana up very thinly – you do not need to mash it as it will break down and disintegrate when you cook it – and layer on top of the spread • Dot mixture with a little butter • In a small bowl mix the beaten egg with a teaspoon of milk • Use a pastry brush to brush egg mixture on the border of pastry • Fold each pastry into a triangle, enclosing the filling, and crimp edges with a fork • Brush the tops of the pastries with more of the egg wash • Cut a couple of small steam vents in the top of each turnover • Place the pastries in the oven and bake for 20 minutes, or until puffed and golden • Serve warm but not hot

Creampie

A Deep South Banana Cream Pie laced with vanilla and sprinkled with chocolate and nutmeg

Creampie is a favourite for those who like it messy - more specifically, if you like to see cream seeping everywhere, this is the pudding for you.

Now, it's worth noting that filming your creampie and sticking it up on the internet can prove a popular way of driving web traffic – Creampies have a loyal following amongst certain online communities on sites like YouPud, PudHub and PudBus.

Strange as it may seem, the sight of a delicious dairy dollop escaping from a sweet pie is something some people use to get themselves off, to sleep. And for those who also like watching 'squirting', just substitute the whipping cream for instant squirty cream.

You will need

¾ cup sugar
⅓ cup plain flour
¼ teaspoon salt
2 cups milk
3 egg yolks, beaten
3 tbsp butter
1 tbsp vanilla essence
4 ripe bananas, sliced
1 ready-baked 9 inch pie crust
1 tbsp white sugar
250ml whipped cream
Grated nutmeg
50g milk chocolate, grated

SERVES 6

Let's get messy

Pre-heat oven to 175c • Combine sugar, flour and salt in a pan; gradually stir in milk and thicken over a medium heat • Stir one cup of mixture into beaten egg yolks in a mixing bowl then immediately add to the rest of the hot mixture in pan. Stir and cook for a further two minutes • Remove from heat and add butter and vanilla and stir until smooth • Slice your bananas and place into your pastry base, and then cover with pudding mixture • Bake for 15 minutes then chill for an hour, OK guy? • Mix sugar with whipping cream and top pie with the cream, and gratings of nutmeg and chocolate

Eat My Mess

An all time classic British dessert with an anarchic twist

Traditional and delectable, the Eton Mess is a strawberry fool that has become a favourite of the chattering classes.
But sometimes we all feel like getting a little messy, so with Eat My Mess, there are no rules, other than it must contain meringue.

Of course, Etonians will know a thing or two about being twisted: usually, this dessert is served only on the 4th of June, at the famous old school. But I say, serve this dish whenever you like - and it's not compulsory for you or your guests to dress up as a schoolboy, bend over and sing Ave Maria in a high voice.

You will need

250g of ready-made meringue
400ml crème fresh
1 tsp sugar
400g strawberries
300ml whipping cream

SERVES 4-6

Let's get messy

Take all the ingredients and put in a mixing bowl (leaving one strawberry untouched) • Mash them with a potato masher or fork until you have created a sweet mess • Top the thing off with a whole strawberry • Pay your dues to the head of the house

Fudge Me Up Against A Wall

A mountain of warm sweet fudge slammed up against a 'wall' of concrete cake

A quick and dirty dessert, something for the al fresco diner. There's nothing quite as basic and animalistic as a dollop of sweet and creamy melted fudge as it is slammed hard up against a wall of concrete (cake).

Wham! Look how the fudge is almost shocked as it hits the wall and you plunge your little spoon into its softness.

Honestly, you are a disgusting diner, you really are.

You will need

300g Devon fudge
200g plain flour
200g sugar
100g butter
50g cocoa powder

SERVES 6

Let's get messy

Mix the flour, sugar and cocoa powder in a bowl •
Melt the butter • Mix it together. Use your fingers -
don't be scared • Grease a tin and pour the mixture
into it • Bake it for about 20 minutes • When you
pull it out, sprinkle your sugar onto it • Melt fudge in
a pan and pour it onto one side of the dish, next to
the "wall" of concrete cake

Serving fudgestion

If you like it hard, leave it to "rest" for a while.
Some people like it soft. Those people are not
to be trusted

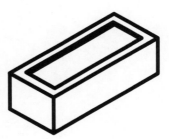

Get Your Gums Round My Plums

**Freshest plums, stewed
with sugared Wine Gums**

Sometimes it's good to try something new. Sometimes you need to throw caution to the wind, order something truly unthinkable online, and hold it front of your partner saying, "I want to do this. And I want to do it to/with/on/using you".

My thinking was, my plums, when at their most ripe and swollen, look as tasty a mouthful as anything on God's earth. It's nature's sweet bounty at its most glorious. Beware though, the taste that actually spews forth from these veiny fruit sacks is often a sour and gloopy affair. To avoid this, stroke and squeeze your plums before they are called into action. If they feel hard, then dampen, soften and warm them up with the torrents of hot juice that flow forth naturally from the gum - this is guaranteed to bring out the sugar. Good luck!

You will need

800g plums, peeled and pitted
A cinnamon stick
½ cup water
5 tbsp granulated sugar
200g wine gums
500ml custard

SERVES 4-6

Let's get messy

Add the cinnamon and sugar to the water and bring to boil • Add the plums and boil again then reduce to simmer for about 10 minutes • Caremelise your wine gums and add to the plums for the final five minutes of cooking • Serve with custard and/or cream

Plum disclaimer

This sounds fun and delicious, but I have no idea what it actually tastes like, as obviously I've never cooked it. If you eat this, you do so at your own risk and the publisher of Fifty Shades Of Gravy cannot be held responsible for the consequences.

Ten Food Related Porn Film Spin Offs

We Need To Pork About Kevin
He's a horrible child and while it may not solve anything…

Full Metal Dildo And A Jacket Potato
War is hell. Dinner is simple

Field of Creams
Biscuits and orgies are on the menu in this feelgood classic set in the sexy world of baseball

The Sure Wank Concoction
Prison gets a lot harder for Tim Robbins and Morgan Freeman. Get busy living, or get busy frying

The Silence of the Lamb Cannons
A sexy gay serial killer romp set in a deaf school

Spotted Dick Tracy
A private dick with a rotten knob

Hot Cock Time Machine
Step back in time to the 80s and get maximum cock

Wallace And Gromit Eat Wensleydale And Pay For An Escort
Gromit rolls his eyes as Wallace calls a prostitute and goes all wrong in his trousers

Die Hard With A Vegan
John McClane turns over a new leaf, and then makes a meal out of it

When Harry's Meat Met Sally
I'll have what she's having. With chips

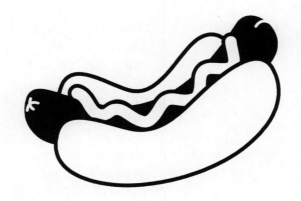

Grunt
And
Cream

A peach and pear 'grunt'
(or cobbler) served with lightly
whipped cream

This is such a primal, earthy way of finishing
off: no frills, straight to the point, wham,
bam, thank you mam. Irresistible.

No-one would claim it's sophisticated, it's
not something you'd use to impress a new
love, or your mum, and there's nothing
complicated about it (it can be over in
seconds): but if anyone, even your mum in
fact, tells you that Grunt and Cream is a
combination that doesn't appeal to them
once in a while, they're lying.

That's right – mummy's telling fibs.

You will need

750g washed, peeled and roughly chopped
fresh or tinned fruit, try peaches,
pears, apples and blackberries
225g self-raising flour, sifted
½ tsp salt
110g butter, cut into small squares
150ml milk
1tbsp sugar

SERVES 6

Let's get messy

Place fruit in the bottom of a baking dish •
Combine the flour, salt, and butter and blend
(by hand or in a mixer) until you have a
breadcrumb-thick mix • Add milk and blend again
until you have a thick, sticky dough • Dish this
mixture onto the fruit – it should look like a
slapdash crumble • Sprinkle sugar on top, and
bake for 30 minutes or until golden and bubbling

Fun food fact!

Grunt is an America version of Cobbler.
You could even 'complete the circle' by offering
it to a cobbler. Agree a price for the mending of
the shoes first though.

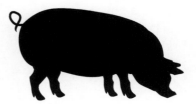

Happy Ending

Endive tarte tatin

One of the things that makes a happy ending 'happy' is its unexpectedness - and this is an unexpected ending if ever there was one, as you finish off with a surprisingly bittersweet treat.

On the one hand, this will leave you feeling ecstatic. But a happy ending or a slice of any tart you probably shouldn't be partaking in is never going to be genuinely nourishing, and feelings of emptiness, guilt and self-doubt may soon creep in.

A coping strategy – e.g. going to church, tidying the shed, helping an old lady across the road – is worth considering in advance.

You will need

1 sheet puff pastry, thawed if frozen
8 tbsp salted butter, plus more for the pan
1 ¾ cups sugar
1 tsp vanilla extract
6 heads Belgian endive,
trimmed and halved vertically
2 tbsp lemon juice
1 egg, lightly beaten with
2 teaspoons water
(for egg wash)

SERVES 6

Let's get messy

Pre-heat oven to 190c • Heat a 12-inch cast iron skillet over medium heat; add butter and once melted, add sugar and vanilla, stir and cook until sugar melts and turns light gold • Pack the endive halves into the caramel cut side down and sprinkle on the lemon juice • Bake covered for 20 minutes, turn endives over and bake uncovered for another 20 minutes • Remove endives and set aside • Butter a 23cm ovenproof skillet and arrange endives in the bottom • Boil the leftover caramel and endive sauce for a few minutes, adding sugar to taste and reducing to the thickness of cough syrup, add to endive pan and top off with a 25cm disc of the pastry, lightly brushed with egg wash, and with four small air vents cut in the pastry • Bake until pastry is puffed and golden, about 20 to 25 minutes • Cool about 10 minutes before inverting onto a plate and serving with vanilla ice cream

Jam Rags Leading To Blue Balls, Bourneville Boulevard And Instant Cream

A bed of ripped jam sponge atop scoops of blue ice cream balls, a motorway-smooth layer of chocolate fudge, finished off with multiple pumps of squirty cream

This is an extremely complex and ultimately messy dessert, but you are almost inevitably going to come across it once in your life.

It all starts with jam rags, leaving everyone feeling slightly unsatisfied, and wondering where they can go from there to salvage the situation. Blue balls on their own can be a frustrating dish to make, but when those blue balls melt as you enter Bourneville Boulevard, and then you reap the benefit of that instant explosion of cream, it makes the mission and the mess more than worth your while.

You will need

500g pot of good-quality vanilla custard
284ml carton double cream
1 tsp blue food colouring
400g dark chocolate 50-70%
400g condensed milk
25g butter
100g icing sugar
One raspberry/strawberry sponge cake
Squirty cream

SERVES 6

Let's get messy

Mix custard, double cream and colouring in a bowl and freeze for about 90 mins until it starts to freeze around the edges • Stir well then repeat process twice until the mix is smooth and frozen • Break chocolate into small pieces and place in a non-stick pan with milk and butter • Melt ingredients gently, stirring until smooth • Sieve in icing sugar and mix thoroughly • Spoon your Bourneville Boulevard of fudge into the bottom of a 20 cm square tin lined with baking paper • Chill in the fridge for 1 hour until set and then pull out of tin, remove baking paper and place fudge in the bottom of a deep serving dish of a similar size • Use an ice cream scoop to cover your Boulevard with Blue Balls • Rip your sponge, cover your balls, and top off with a thick layer of squirty cream

Knob Cheese Cake

A deliciously tangy and fragrant cheese cake with a crumbly Dorset Knob biscuit base

Who can forget their first delicious taste of a Dorset Knob? You were probably on holiday, and had parked up in a lay-by a few miles from Durdle Door to escape the rain. You wound down your window to take a peek outside and then boink – you'd been persuaded to take a Knob in your mouth.

I bet like me you loved your first 'taste of the country' and were soon gobbling away. Even now though, it takes a leap of faith, because it still sounds a bit funny on paper. I like cake, yeah, and I like cheese, and I love Knob. But together? Surely not? But it does work; and now I've even added Ginger Nuts to help create a mouthful of Knobs and Nuts you will never forget.

Cook this and you will have a great chance of 'getting off with' your guests.

You will need

100g Dorset Knob biscuits
100g digestive biscuits
50g Ginger Nut biscuits
100g melted butter
600g soft cheese
100g icing sugar
Vanilla seeds
285ml double cream
Fresh berries
Sugar syrup
Cream

SERVES 6

Let's get messy

Butter and line a 20cm tin with baking parchment •
Seal biscuits in a plastic food bag and crush to
crumbs with a rolling pin • Transfer the crumbs to
a mixing bowl and pour over the melted butter and
mix thoroughly • Tip the mixture into your tin,
smooth out and chill in the fridge until base is set
(approx 60 mins) • Beat soft cheese, icing sugar
and vanilla until smooth and then pour in cream
and beat until combined • Spoon mixture into tin
and leave to set overnight • Bring it to room
temperature, place the base on top of a plate,
slowly pull the sides of the tin down, slip the cake
onto a serving plate, then remove the lining paper
and base • Top with fresh strawberries, sugar syrup
and cream

Fun Food Presentation Idea #3 Knickerbocker Glory Hole

A sexually powerful recipe from the United States of Ooh Yeah Baby. The KBGH is for those of you with a more adventurous outlook, the glory hole being like a sexy, food-based version of Russian Roulette. What will come through the hole next? Will it be nuts, whipped cream or soft strawberry? Or will it be a Knickerbocker Glory?

The hardest thing about the Knickerbocker Glory itself seems to be getting your hands on a suitably tall, sundae glass. A pint glass will suffice however in this recipe, as the beauty of the glory hole is that the person consuming can't see what's coming their way until it's waaaay too late.

Trickier still, is organising your glory hole. If you're in the mood for something quick, why not use a piece of cardboard / chipboard. You can find these at all good DIY shops or glory hole suppliers.

You will need

A wall or piece of chipboard
Tall sundae or pint glass
A sprinkling of nuts
2 scoops of ice cream
2 tbsp of cream
1 crushed meringue
1 tbsp whipped cream
1 cherry
1 dessert spoon of assorted fruit
(kiwi, strawberry, banana)
Fruit sauce
A long spoon

Create your hole

You will need a large sharp knife and a piece of plasterboard or a wall • Select waist high area to cut • Cut hole approximately 5 inches in diameter

Make your glory

Chop the fruit up into small pieces • Put into bottom of glass • Add a scoop of ice cream Pour in some fruit sauce • Add in some crumbled up meringue • Some cream now • More sauce • Whipped cream at top • Sprinkle some nuts • Top it off with a cherry

How to eat it

Position the "eater" on one side of the glory hole, and tell them to "stand by". As you see their eye appear at the hole, request they "open wide". Then it's up to you as "the feeder" what happens next…

Why not give it that public toilet feel by urinating on the kitchen floor a few days before and smashing all the mirrors in the house.

Musty Split Peach Covered In Banana Yoghurt

Over-ripened peach halves
with fermented juice, banana
and yoghurt

A ripe banana, a musty split peach, a yoghurt explosion – to me, this is the Holy Trinity of desserts, and it's as much about the presentation as anything.

But if you don't want to waste your yoghurt on a peach, then dip some onto the end of your banana and lower it into your mouth and down your throat (being careful not to gag, as this can be off-putting); then gently ease the banana out so that the now moistened tip rests against your lips. Then lick the yoghurt off the tip in a slow circular motion.

You will need

3 over-ripe peaches
(easier than making fermented peach 'must')
6 bananas, peeled but firm
12 grapes
Plain yoghurt

SERVES 6

Let's get messy

Split your peaches into halves and de-stone •
Lay one half of each split peach on a flat dessert
dish, flesh side up. Place a banana with one end
pointing into the crevice of the split peach, the
other resting on the plate • Garnish the plate end
of the banana with two grapes, and cover the
peach end, and the split peach itself, with the
creamy yoghurt

Spooning tip

Invite your guests to eat their own the same way,
but provide some spoons in case anyone 'gets
weird' about it.

Pump-Me Pie With Passion

Delicious pumpkin pie served with fresh passion fruit

Pump, pump, pump, pump, pump, pump, more passion, come on, pump, pump, pump, pump, pump. Every Christmas, my wife surprises me with the fervour with which she demands her annual Pump-Me Pie. "Pump Me Pie With Passion," she says to me beforehand in a thick Yorkshire accent, pointing a gnarled and threatening finger in my face.

Like everything, the Americans think they invented this, but as I always say, nobody does it better than me and my missus, so why should it be any different for you (with your own partner)?

Good luck all!

You will need

1 edible pumpkin/butternut squash
145g maple syrup
1 tsp cinnamon
½ tsp ground ginger
½ tsp ground cloves
2 large eggs, beaten
150ml evaporated milk
Thawed frozen puff pastry to line a 20cm tart tin
6 passion fruit
Double cream

SERVES 6

Let's get messy

Pre-heat the oven to 200c • Cut pumpkin/squash into quarters, remove seeds and stringy bits and roast skin side up for 35 mins or until tender • Remove from oven; when cooled, remove flesh and blend in a processor until smooth • Place in a sieve and drain for an hour to remove all liquid • Spoon 250g of your pumpkin purée into a large bowl and stir in maple syrup and spices • Taste, then mix in eggs and gradually stir in evaporated milk until thick and creamy • Use your pastry to line a buttered 20cm tart tin and pour your mixture into the pastry case • Bake for about 35 minutes or until the filling is set but wobbles • Allow to cool on a wire rack for an hour • Scoop the seeds, flesh and juice out of the passion fruit and serve atop the pie with double cream

Soggy Biscuit

A right royal Eton Mess with shortbread

I haven't had this since I was at Radley/Clayesmore/Stowe" is the usual delighted refrain that rings forth at a supper party when I run into the kitchen and shout "Soggy Biscuit" at my guests.

As synonymous with private education as unnecessary ball checks by the school doctor, my version of Soggy Biscuit is essentially a re-cum-structed Eton Mess: strawberries, cream and then shortbread biscuit rather than meringue, with the biscuit made oh so soggy from any gloops of cream you can find.

In fact, you can even make a game of it: ask each of your guests to contribute some cream; last person to dredge some up has to down the whole lot.

You will need

400g strawberries
1 packet of shortbread biscuits,
smashed up
500ml softly whipped cream
A dash of sugar
A dash of port

SERVES 6

Let's get messy

Mash strawberries with a little sugar and port, and fold in broken biscuits and whipped cream

Fun public school food fact!

Apparently, playing soggy biscuit (like shoving a Mars Bar up your anus as part of a rugby club initiation) does NOT make you gay.

Squirt Cream In A Johnny

An American 'Johnnycake' pancake filled with maple syrup and squirty cream

Squirt Cream in a Johnny? Not one for the purists this, who would say I was taking all the pleasure out of the dish entirely by denying you your full cream rights.

But I think there's a real retro pleasure to this: it reminds me of sneaking off behind the village hall at parties when I was sixteen, with literally anyone who'd let me squirt my cream in their pancake.

And if that sounds cheap, don't be fooled – maple syrup has risen in price considerably in recent years, thanks to unpredictable weather patterns affecting production levels (not a joke).

You will need

4 cups polenta or maize flour
2 tbsp sugar
2 tsp salt
1 cup milk
4 cups boiling water
Butter

SERVES 6

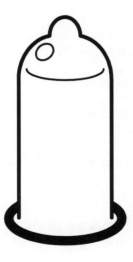

Let's get messy

Whisk cornmeal, sugar and salt • Pour in boiling water and mix into a paste • Stir in milk, remembering you don't want this runnier than creamy mash • Melt 1 tbsp butter into a pan and spoon batter in to make 2-inch pancakes •
Cook for 4 mins each side until browned, and then remove and start a new pancake • Serve stacked up with a massive flood of cream and maple syrup

Serving suggestion

You could deliver this with the lovely line, "let's get dirty squirty". Or you could not bother.

Brilliant New Ideas For Food-Based Sexual Euphemisms

Let's boil some eggs, yeah?

I feel like folding in some cream

It's Sunday – how about I stick this beef in and leave it for a couple of hours?

Do you mind if I rinse my potatoes in your Belfast sink? (Only really useable with a Northern Irish girl)

Oooh, yeah, I wanna ferment your yeast

Let's see what's in the fridge

Shall we brown the beef?

Fruit salad? How about you peel the banana while I squeeze the plums?

Fancy some dressing on those?

Do you want some of my pie?

Does this sausage smell off to you?

Swiss Role Play With An Accidental Finger Of Fudge

A Swiss roll with a melted Finger of Fudge centre

Many of my favourite recipe creations have come about accidentally, and this, as the name suggests, is one of them.

One day my wife and I were indulging in some Swiss Role Play - I wanted her to give me some sugar, and she was perfectly willing to help, but as we become entangled in our rather modestly proportioned galley kitchen, I slipped, and ended up with a Finger of Fudge. But do you know what? She loved it!

And so this delicious dessert dish was born – a visual treat, where the juxtaposition of the creamy white sponge makes its fudgey centre look just like a bum-hole.

You will need

3 small-medium eggs
75g caster sugar
75g self-raising flour
Two Fingers of Fudge
75g strawberry jam
125ml whipped double cream
Icing sugar

SERVES 6

Let's get messy

Pre-heat oven to 190c • Whisk eggs and sugar together, fold in flour and spoon mixture into a greased and lined 23 x 30cm Swiss Roll tin • Bake in oven for 10 minutes • Add Fingers of Fudge to the far left hand side of the flat sponge and then replace into oven for a further 2-5 mins or until sponge is light but springy and fudge has started to melt • Remove from oven, sprinkle some caster sugar on a square of baking paper and turn cake out onto paper, gently removing original paper and tin • Spread jam evenly onto top of sponge, and then the cream on top of that • Roll, and then sprinkle the outside with icing sugar • Your fudge centre will look like a bum-hole and the cake is ready to be served

Uncle Keith's Weeping Spotted Dick

A classic Spotted Dick infused with a raspberry jus

For many, like my Uncle Keith, a spotted dick is a comfort – testament to a life of excess, lived to the full, with a healthy and unstinting appetite for pleasure and sensual gratification, and a chance to celebrate all this expansively with some custard.

Uncle Keith's Weeping Spotted Dick takes this recipe to the next level, as a potent, florid blood-red juice oozes and mushrooms from the centre of the dick like a rabid, toxic infection.

Call the doctor – this dish is TOO de-lish.

You will need

50g butter
300g plain flour
3 tsp baking powder
150g shredded suet
1 tbsp golden syrup
80g golden caster sugar
100g currants
50g raisins
Grated zest of 1 lemon
75 ml milk
75 ml whipping cream
Custard

SERVES 6

Let's get messy

Butter a 1.4 litre pudding basin • Combine the flour, baking powder, suet, syrup, sugar and dried fruit in a large bowl and then melt the remaining butter and stir into the flour mixture • Add lemon zest • Combine the milk and cream in a small jug and stir into the mixture until it is thick but pourable • Pour the mixture into the pudding basin • Cover with greaseproof paper tied in place with string • Place the basin in a steamer basket set over boiling water and steam until cooked • Should be 60-70 minutes but check the water level regularly • Serve with custard

Two-for-the-price-of-one alternative recipe

Brown Weeping Spotted Dick
(as above but with chocolate)

Wet The Bed With A Golden Shower

A springy bed of sponge moistened with a sticky shower of golden syrup

There's nothing quite like a splash of gold to moisten a velvety smooth sheet of icing sugar atop the firm but fluffy resistance of a luxurious bed of sponge.

I once went 18 months without sponge and I grew to crave its conservative vanilla rewards, like a prisoner bored of the sight of his thick, guilt-inducing morning porridge. When release finally came and I was granted sponge in all its moist, feathery glory, I quickly craved something more elaborate – namely for my bed to be bathed in a steaming golden shower.

It's recommended that you wash your hands and face afterwards at the very least. You may even need a bath.

You will need

200g butter
200g golden syrup
300g self-raising flour
1 tsp salt
200g muscovado sugar
3 eggs, beaten
2 tbsp milk
Icing sugar
Custard

SERVES 6

Let's get messy

Pre-heat the oven to 170c • Butter and line base of a Swiss Roll tin with baking paper • Melt butter and 150g of golden syrup in a saucepan, stirring to combine • Cool for 15-20 minutes • Sift the flour with the salt and stir in the sugar • Beat in cooled syrup mixture • Beat eggs and milk, then combine with flour mixture until smooth • Pour into tin, smooth out and bake for 40 minutes or until a skewer comes out clean • Quickly warm up rest of syrup, sprinkle icing sugar on cake and then drizzle on the warm syrup and serve with multiple pumps of custard

Fun food tip!

Mess your bed still further with choccy streaks and jammy smears

The Edible
Dildo Scale

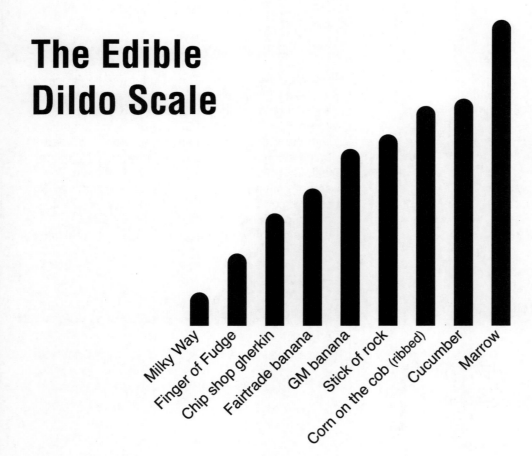

Milky Way
Finger of Fudge
Chip shop gherkin
Fairtrade banana
GM banana
Stick of rock
Corn on the cob (ribbed)
Cucumber
Marrow

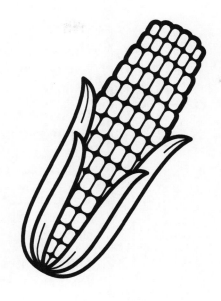

Acknowledgements

Thanks first and foremost must go to the creative genius that is Delme. His patience, artistic flair and constant stream of abuse kept the book on track and me on my toes.

Thanks to Jo for her support, Alisha for her love and ideas and to Keith for his continued insanity.

To Gareth for his advice and Gordon for his inspiration (those long windy walks on the Dales discussing Sartre and the Third World debt really helped me forget my troubles).

To the podcast I Am Idiot for its insight, irresponsible claims and dogged pursuit of stupidity.

And of course to Nigella. You are the spur, the benchmark, the slippery yardstick. I love you.

About The Author

I M Pliant grew up in the small Yorkshire town of Curmudgeon, and always had a flair for language and cookery.

After graduating from the Battenberg School of Cuisine in Lewisham, I M worked at some of London's most celebrated restaurants and eating establishments.

He lives in North London with his wife Emmental and their children Flora and Lurpak.

8733841R00078

Printed in Great Britain
by Amazon.co.uk, Ltd.,
Marston Gate.